ULTIMATE KEYBOARD PLAY-ALONG

Pink Floyd

Play Along with 9 Great-Sounding Tracks

Alfred

Alfred Publishing Co., Inc.
16320 Roscoe Blvd., Suite 100
P.O. Box 10003
Van Nuys, CA 91410-0003
alfred.com

ISBN-10: 0-7390-5939-4 (Book & CD)
ISBN-13: 978-0-7390-5939-5 (Book & CD)

Pink Floyd

Play Along with 9 Great-Sounding Tracks

Contents

CD recorded at the Mews Recording Studios, London
www.themewsrecordingstudios.com
Dave Clarke, recording and mix engineer
Tom Fleming, guitars
Neil Williams, bass
Darrin Mooney, drums
Alle Pearse, keyboards
Stephen Wilcox, sax
Alison Symons, voice
Children from Gallions School, Newham, choir

Compiled by Matt Smith, Tom Fleming, and Olly Weeks
Book edited by Lucy Holliday and Olly Weeks
Music arranged and engraved by Tom Fleming

Cover photograph: © Michael Ochs Archives/Getty Images

ANOTHER BRICK IN THE WALL
(Part 2)

Words and Music by ROGER WATERS

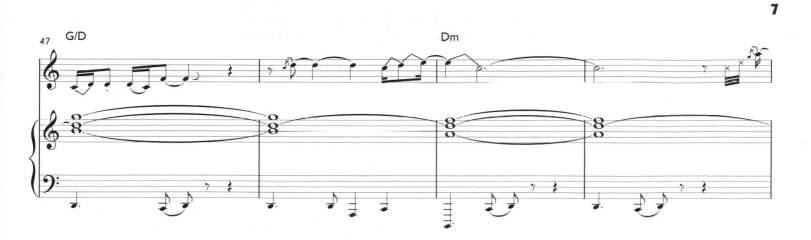

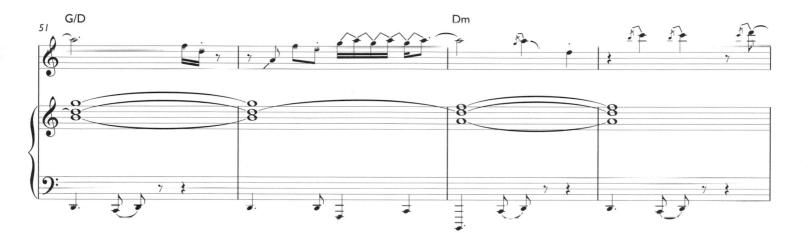

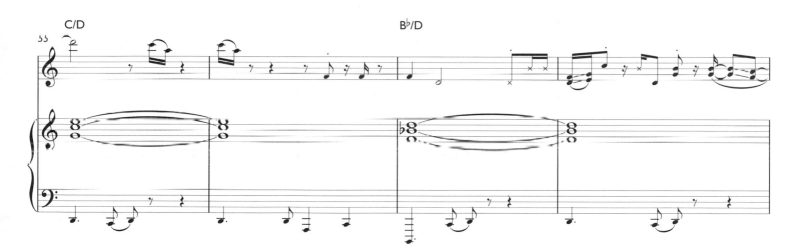

Another Brick in the Wall (Part 2) - 4 - 4
32183

COMFORTABLY NUMB

Words and Music by ROGER WATERS and DAVID GILMOUR

Re- lax.

I'll need some in - for - ma - tion first.____

Just the bas - ic facts.____ Can you show me where it hurts?____

There is____ no pain____ you are____ re - ce - ding.

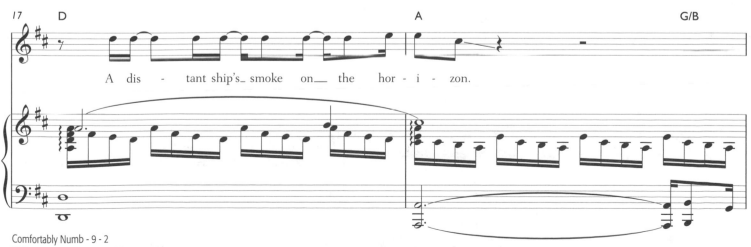

A dis - tant ship's_ smoke on__ the hor - i - zon.

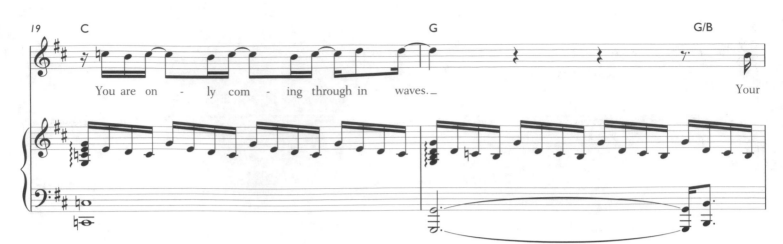

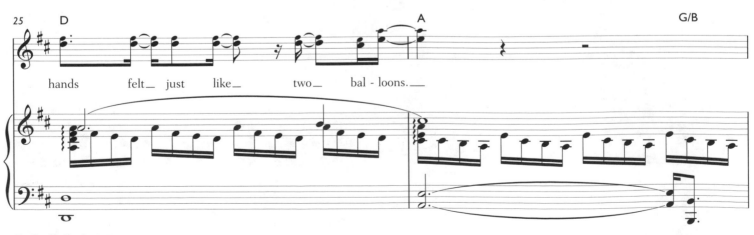

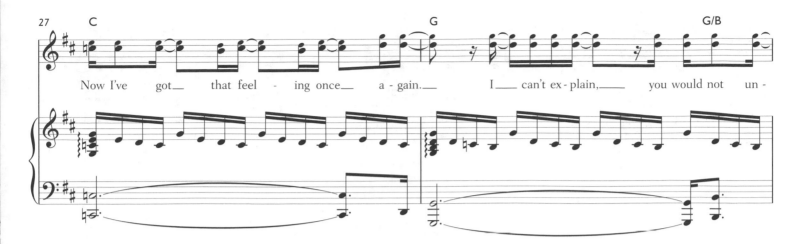

Now I've got__ that feel - ing once__ a - gain.__ I__ can't ex - plain,__ you would not un -

- der - stand,__ this is not how__ I am.__

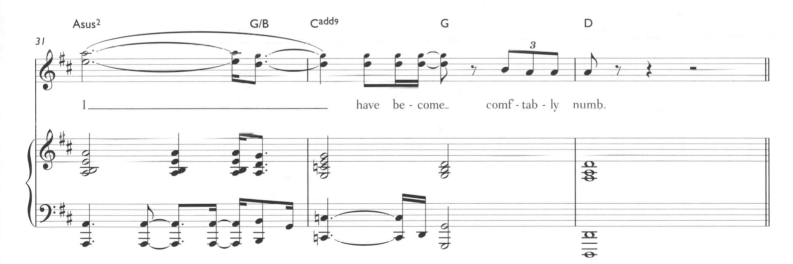

I_____ have be - come__ comf' - tab - ly numb.

(Guitar solo)

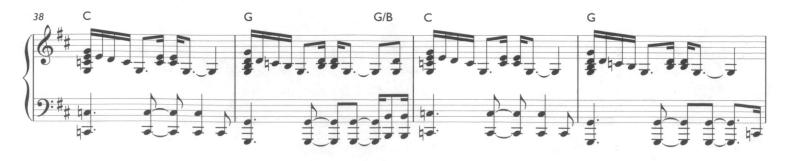

I _____ have be-come_ comf'-tab-ly numb.

O.-K. Just a lit-tle pin-prick. There'll be no more...

(Aaaaah!) _____ But you may feel a lit-tle sick. Can you

stand up? I do be-lieve it's work-ing, good.___ That-'ll keep you

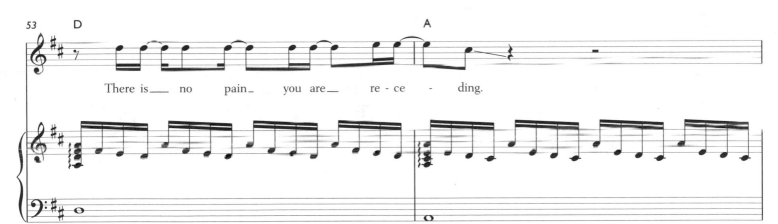

go-ing through the show.___ Come on it's time_ to go.___

There is___ no pain_ you are_ re-ce-ding.

A dis-tant ship's smoke on___ the hor-i-zon.

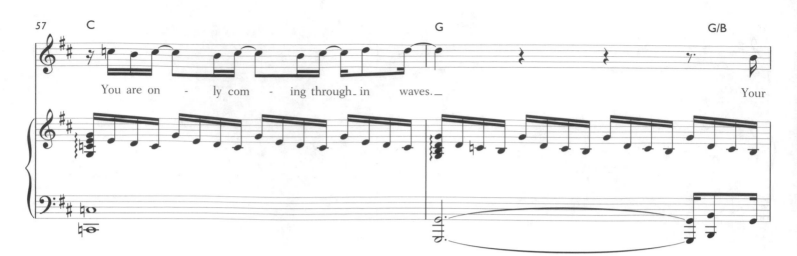

You are on - ly com - ing through in waves.___ Your

lips move___ but I can't hear___ what you're say - ing. When I___

___ was a child I___ caught a fleet - ing glimpse___

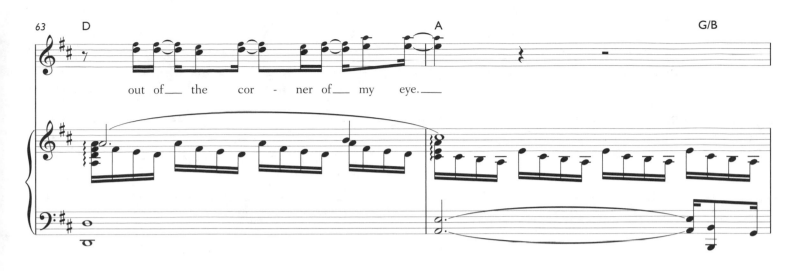

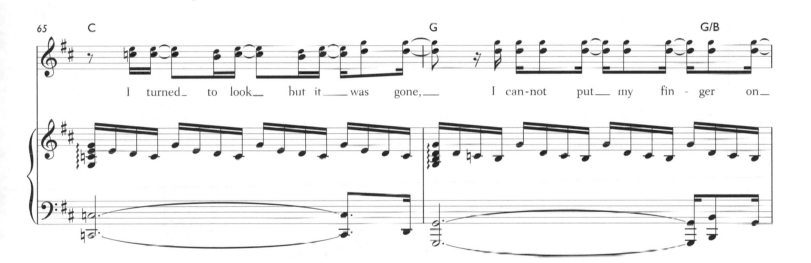

I _____ have be-come comf'-tab-ly numb.

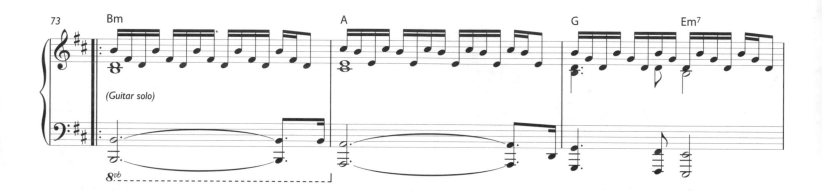

(Guitar solo)

Play section 4x

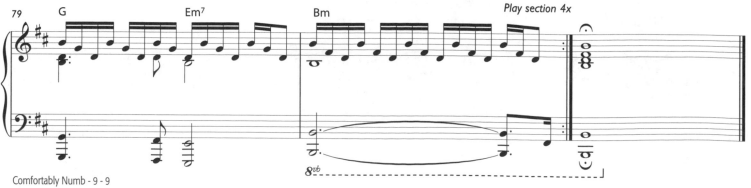

MONEY

Words and Music by ROGER WATERS

2 bars FX loop count in

♩ = 119+ (variable)

(Bass)

1. Mon - ey,   get a - way._____   Get a
2. Mon - ey,   get   back._____   I'm
3. Mon - ey,   it's a crime._____   Share

Money - 7 - 1
32183

18

good job with more pay and you're o - kay. Mon-
all right Jack, keep your hands off of my___ stack. Mon-
it fair - ly but don't take a slice of my___ pie.

- ey,___ it's a gas.___ Grab that cash with both hands and make
- ey,___ it's a hit.___ Don't give me that do good-y good bull-
Mon-ey,___ so they say,___ is the root of all ev - il to-

To Coda ⊕   F#m7

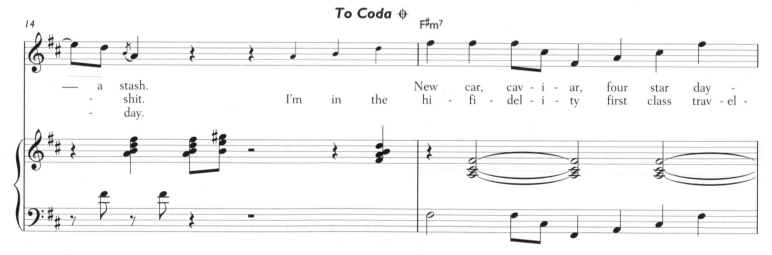

— a stash. New car, cav - i - ar, four star day -
- shit. I'm in the hi - fi - del - i - ty first class trav - el -
- day.

Em7   Bm7

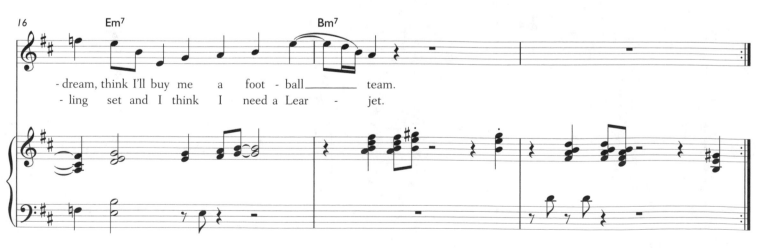

- dream, think I'll buy me a foot - ball___ team.
- ling set and I think I need a Lear - jet.

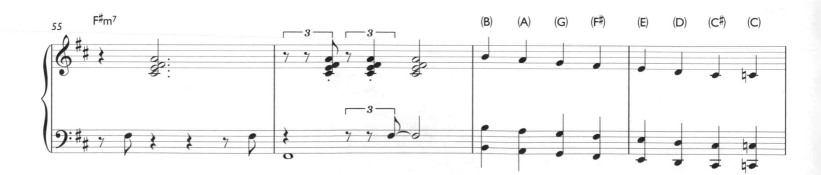

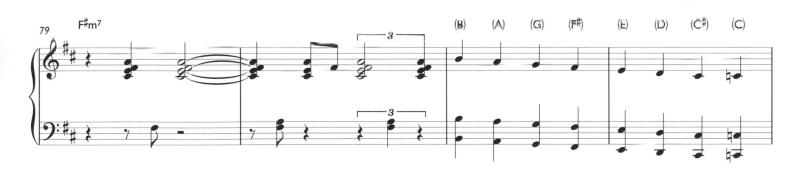

Money - 7 - 5
32183

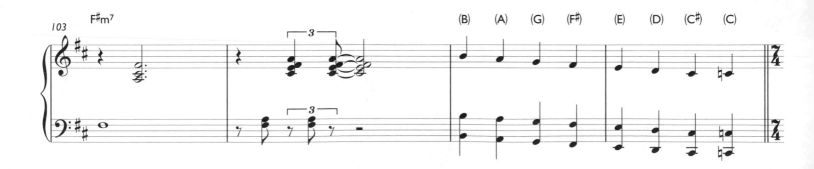

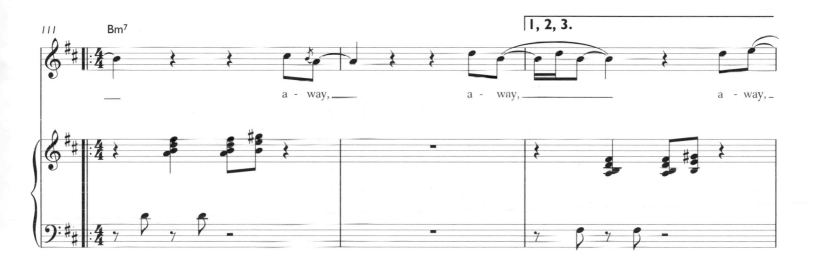

THE FLETCHER MEMORIAL HOME

Words and Music by ROGER WATERS

Take all your ov - er-grown in-fants a-way some - where and build them a home, a lit-tle place of their own, ___ the Flet-cher Mem-or - i - al Home for in - cur-a-ble ty-rants and kings.

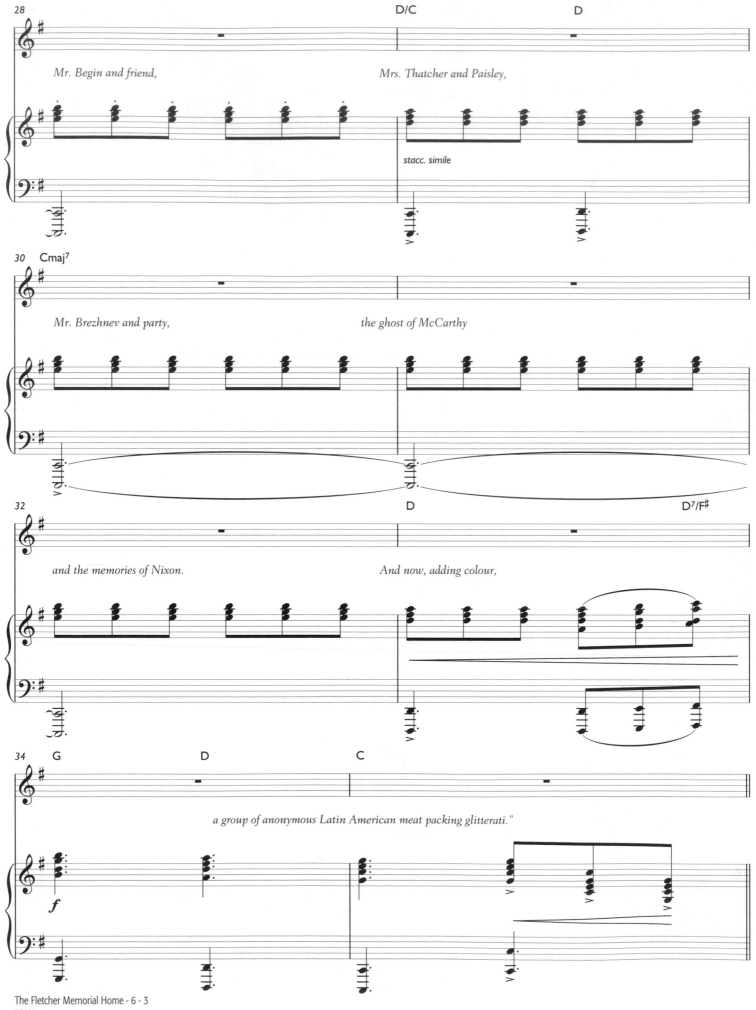

Did they ex-pect us to treat___ them with an-y res-pect? They can
po-lish their med-als and sharp-en their smiles,___ and a-muse them-selves, play-ing games for a while.
Boom boom, bang bang, lie down, you're dead.___

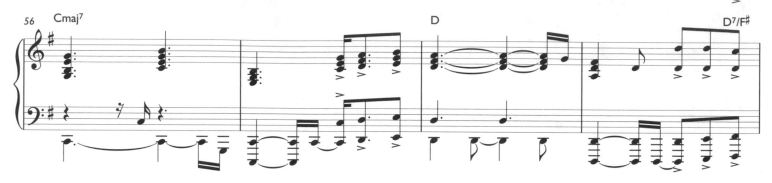

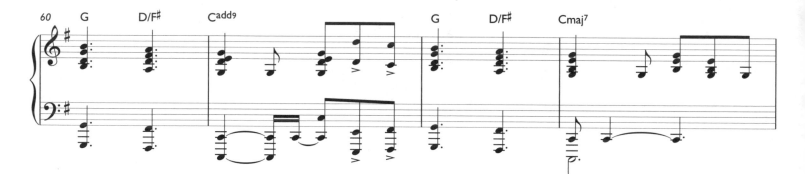

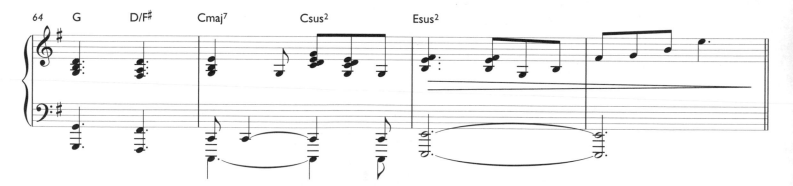

Safe in the per-ma-nent gaze of a cold glass eye,

their fav-our-ite toy, ___ they'll be good girls and boys ___

in the Flet-cher Mem-or- i-al Home for col-o - ni-al

wast- ers of life and limb. Is ev-'ry-one in? Are you

hav-ing a nice time? Now the fin-al ___ sol-u -tion can be ap - plied.

HAVE A CIGAR

Words and Music by ROGER WATERS

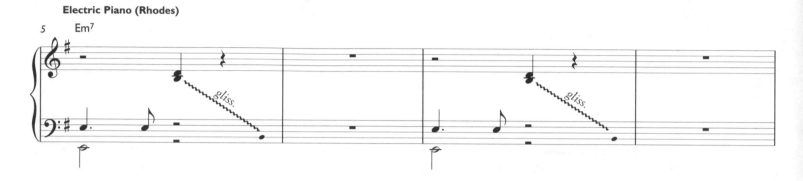

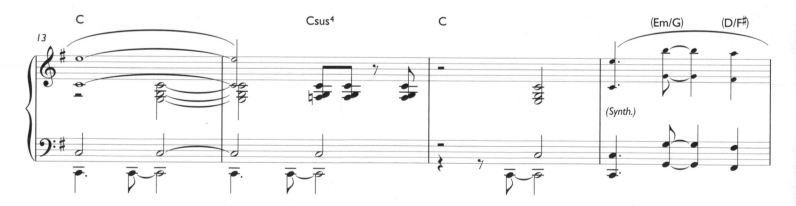

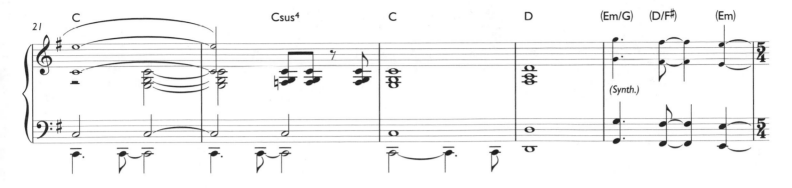

1. Come in here, dear boy, have a ci-gar. You're gon-na go far. You're gon-na
2. We're just knocked out. We heard about the sell out. You

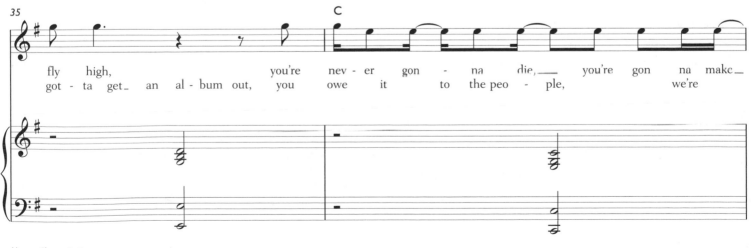

fly high, you're nev-er gon-na die, you're gon-na make
got-ta get an al-bum out, you owe it to the peo-ple, we're

Have a Cigar - 6 - 2
32183

_it if_ you try; they're gon - na love you.
so hap - py we can hard - ly count._____

Well I've al - ways had   a deep res - pect and I mean that most sin - cere - ly.
Ev - 'ry - bo - dy else is   just green;_____ have_

_you seen the chart?   It's a   hell - uv - a   start,__ it could   be made in - to a mon - ster if we

The band   is just fan - tas - tic, that is   real - ly what I think,   oh,__

by the way,   which one's Pink? }
all   pull to - geth - er as a team. }

And did we

tell you the name of the game, boy, we call it Rid-ing the Gra-vy

Train.

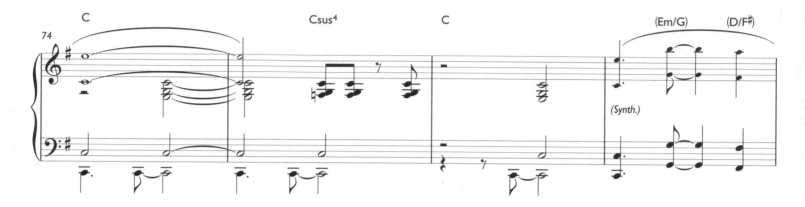

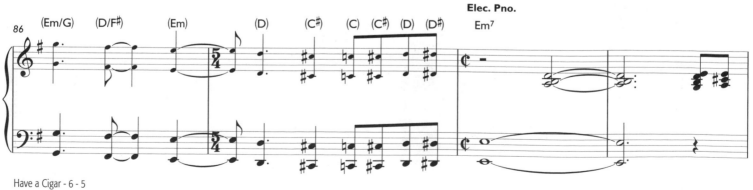

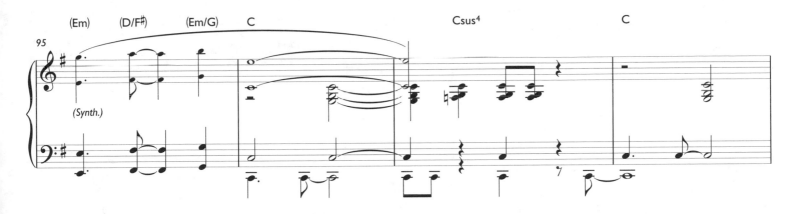

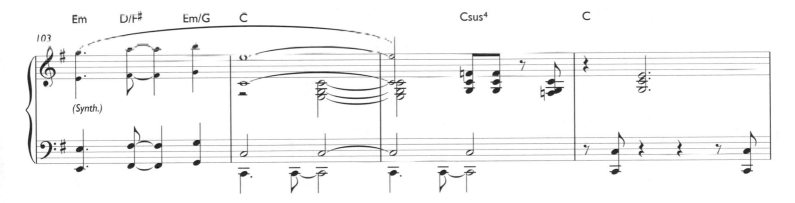

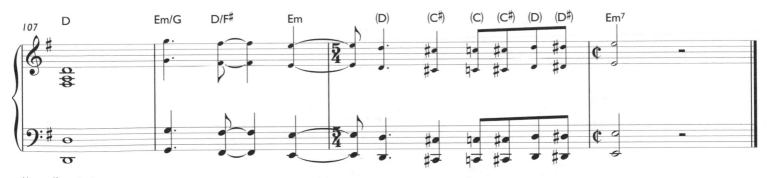

SEE EMILY PLAY

Words and Music by SYD BARRETT

2 bars count in

♩ = 123

1. Em - i - ly tries_ but mis - un - der - stands.
2. Soon af - ter dark_ Em - i - ly cries.___
3. Put on a gown that touch - es the ground.

(Ah - ooh) She's

1. oft - en in - clined_ to bor - row some - bo - dy's dreams_ 'til to - mor - row.___
2. Gaz - ing through trees_ in sor - row, hard - ly a sound_ 'til to - mor - row.___
3. Float on a riv - er for - ev - er and ev - er,_ Em - i - ly.

There is no

(3rd time play 8va higher)

(Electric Guitar w/delay)

(Bass)

See Emily Play - 4 - 1
32183

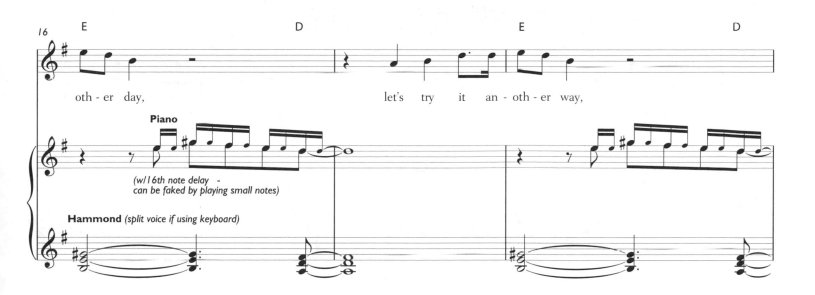

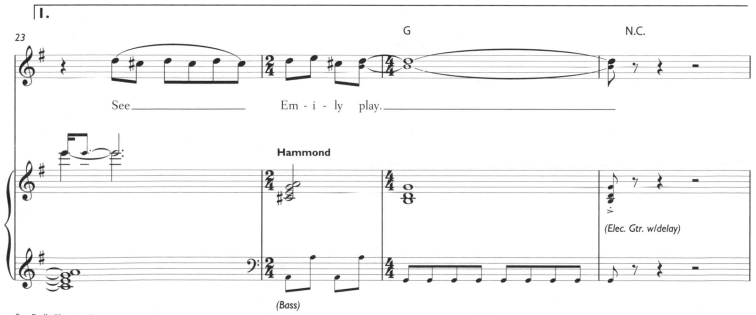

D.S. al Coda   **Coda**

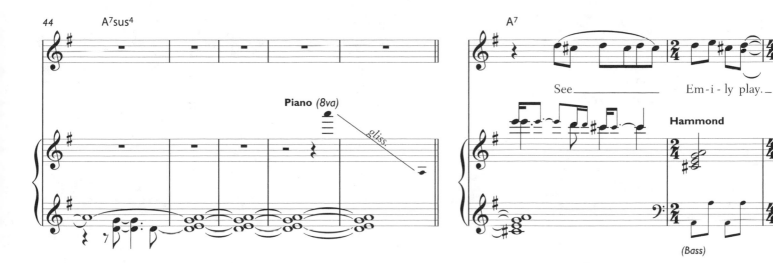

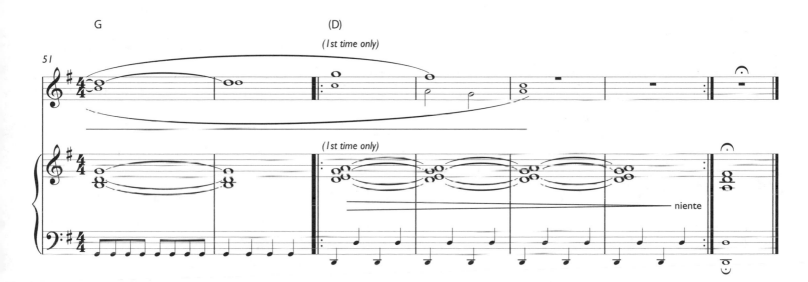

Insert 1 - Recorded by Syd Barrett, Rick Wright and Nick Mason.
The tape was then played at double speed and inserted into the two bars at the end of verse 1

See Emily Play - 4 - 4
32183

TIME

Words and Music by
ROGER WATERS, NICHOLAS MASON, DAVID GILMOUR and RICK WRIGHT

1 bar "tick tock" count in

♩ = 60

Electric Piano (Wurlitzer)

(Bass & Synth.)

TRO – © 1973 (Renewed) HAMPSHIRE HOUSE PUBLISHING CORP., New York, New York
All Rights Reserved   Used by Permission

To Coda ⊕

33 Dmaj7 · · · Amaj7

Tired of ly - ing in___ the sun - shine, stay - ing home___ to watch___ the rain. And
Ev - 'ry year is get - ting short - er, nev - er seem___ to find___ the time.

35 Dmaj7 · · · Aadd9

you are young and life___ is long___ and there is time to kill___ to - day.___
Plans that ei - ther come___ to naught___ or half a page of scrib - bled lines.___

(Backing vocals enter)

37 Dmaj7 · · · C#m

And then one day you find___ ten years have got___ be - hind___ you.
Hang - ing on in qui - et des - per - a - tion is the Eng - lish way,___ the

39 Bm · · · E

No one told you when___ to run,___ you missed the start - ing gun.___

(Guitar solo)

Time - 6 - 4
32183

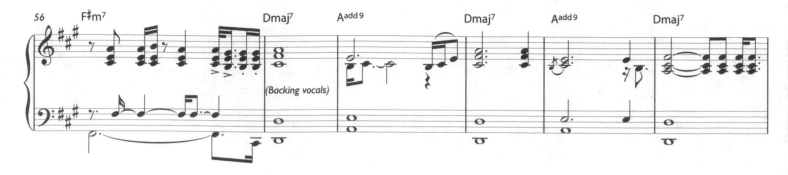

D.S. al Coda

Coda

2. And you run—

time is gone,— the song is ov - er,

thought I'd some-thing more to say.—

Home,— home a - gain.—

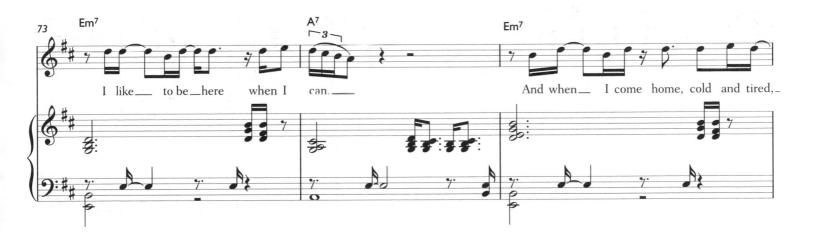

I like___ to be___ here when I can.___ And when___ I come home, cold and tired,___

it's good to warm___ my bones be-side the fire.___

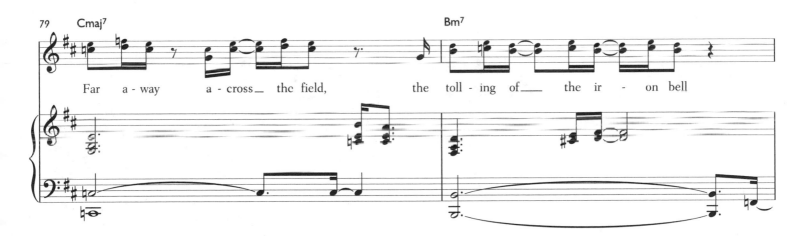

Far a - way a - cross___ the field, the toll - ing of___ the ir - on bell

calls the faith - ful to___ their knees to hear the soft - ly spok - en mag - ic spells.

WISH YOU WERE HERE

Words and Music by ROGER WATERS and DAVID GILMOUR

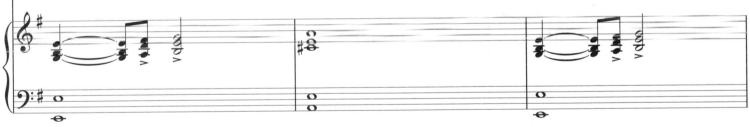

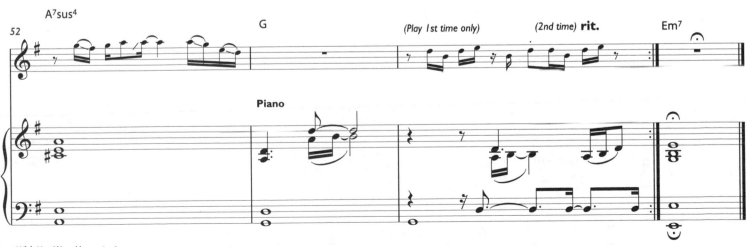

YOUNG LUST

Words and Music by ROGER WATERS and DAVID GILMOUR

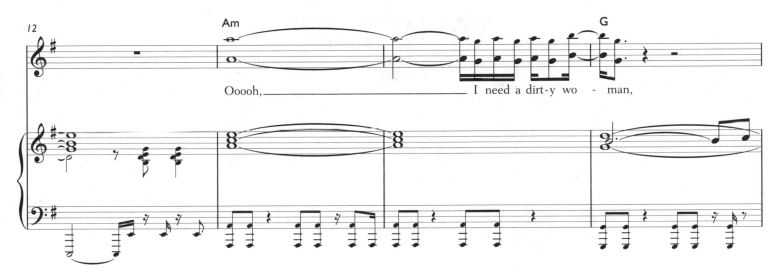

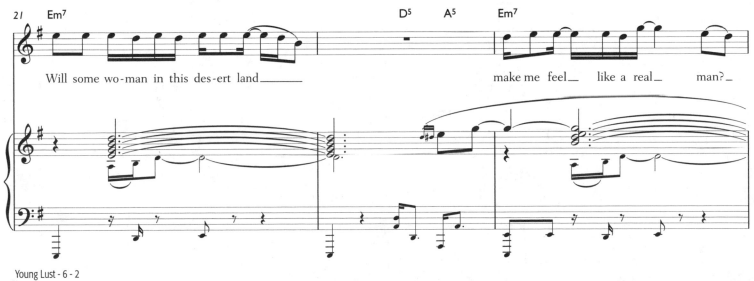

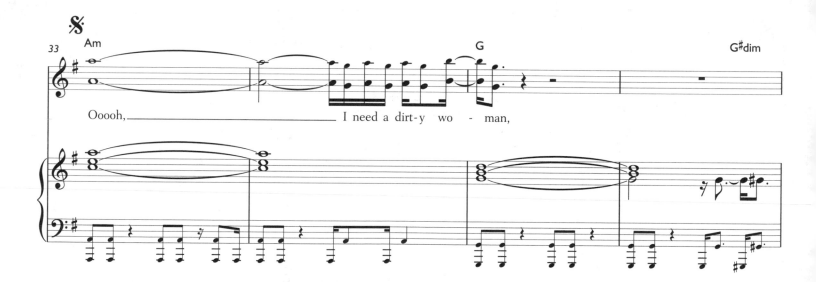

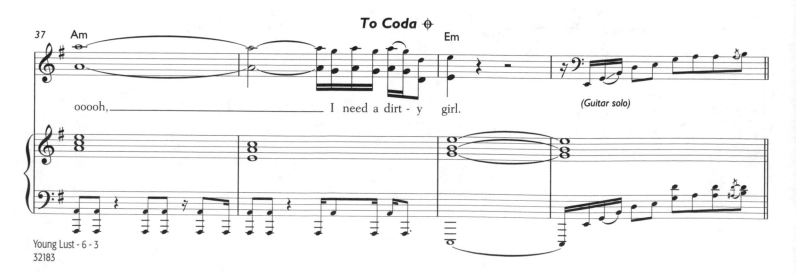

D.S. al Coda   **Coda**

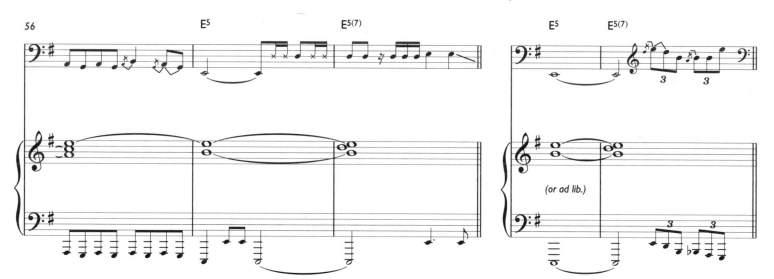

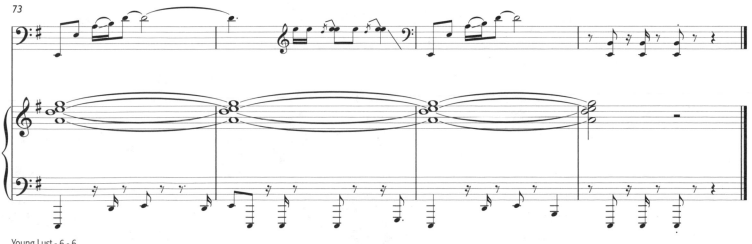